"I Believe in You"

And the Other Top Three Things my Parents Should Have Told Me

Tina Sass

authorHOUSE®

AuthorHouse™
1663 Liberty Drive
Bloomington, IN 47403
www.authorhouse.com
Phone: 1-800-839-8640

First published by AuthorHouse   5/20/2010

ISBN: 978-1-4490-8868-2 (e)
ISBN: 978-1-4490-8870-5 (sc)

Library of Congress Control Number: 2010902540

Printed in the United States of America
Bloomington, Indiana

This book is printed on acid-free paper.

CONTENTS

INTRODUCTION

The original title of this book was to be "four things my parents should have told me." As I talked to people about this book, what became apparent is that there are hundreds of things people wish their parents would have told them. So I say to you, dear readers who have taken the time to open this book, think about something you wish your parents would have told you and TELL your children or young people in your life. Hug them. Ask them a question about themselves and truly listen to their answer. Play a game with them. Tell them they are good at something. A few minutes of positive reinforcement every day could change their lives. Say "I believe in you."

During the course of writing and researching for this book, I realized I am now responsible for the top "four things" I wish I had known. If I continue to blame, I will never get better. If I don't forgive and forget--move on and forward--I will never be the person I want to be or the person I hope to be for others.

Therefore, if I had the chance to go back and "re-do" some key moments of my life, the next four chapters outline these things.

These things have affected ALL aspects of my well being. They have affected my self esteem, my self worth, and nearly all of my daily choices. I struggled for years with what "I should be doing" and what "I should be at my age" and what "I should have financially" and what "I should look like." I have made so many mistakes and taken so many careless actions in life. I wholeheartedly believe that I was only blessed to get through all of it to share the message contained within these pages. I thank God every single day for the angels that have been placed along the path of my life and for all that I have and for all that I am. Cliché as it is, I appreciate every breath of every day, every breeze that blows across my face, every time I feel the warmth of the sun because I was once in a place where the breeze didn't blow and the sun didn't shine.

CHAPTER 1:

AIN'T NO MAN GONNA TAKE CARE OF YOU.

It is an amazing thing to be an American woman. If I stop to think about what it would be like to be a woman in Iraq or Iran or Pakistan, I have nothing to complain about. However, I am an American.

It is a confusing time for women. We are expected to produce financially like a man, have man feelings (God forbid you cry in a meeting), and approach sexuality like a man. At the same time, we are expected to still be lady like, scrub the floor, do the laundry and "rear the young". We are supposed to be two genders at the same time and it is seriously confusing! I was raised by the last generation of "old school". My mom didn't work, she was appreciated for being the stay at home mom. There were four of us...FOUR KIDS...and she still has dinner on the table every night for my dad. Being raised in that environment, I expected to be married with kids by my early twenties—a stay at home mom attending PTA meetings, volunteering and baking. HA!

To this day, when I go home to see my great grandmother, she says, "Just get married and you'll be fine." In 2010, things no longer work like they did fifty years ago. They don't even work like they did twenty years ago! And honey, it is a confusing world us women live in.

I often feel disheartened by this—tired of being solely responsible for myself and my situation. I wouldn't be disheartened if the whole marriage thing hadn't been jammed down my throat. And please, the man I dated at twenty—that magic age where I was supposed to settle down—is COMPLETELY different than the man I look for now at thirty two. So what would have happened if I settled with that guy at twenty? Divorce? Adultery? Obesity? Sadness? I am still learning who I am and what makes ME happy. And sometimes I feel guilty about that. Again, those "rules" I was raised to live by—do this for this person because it is the right thing to do…the right thing for who? For you? Just because it is the right thing for you DOES NOT MEAN it is the right thing for me. And it took me thirty two years of suffering to realize this.

I do believe in love. I do believe in a man who will respect me, care for me, value my wit and intelligence. A man whom I can count on and trust. I do not expect a man to take care of me or be responsible for my financial well being.

What would I share with the young women of America?

So please, women of tomorrow, don't read your daughters Cinderella and Snow White and freaking Rapunzel. I am not negative, I am realistic. We are all just humans, and that is too much pressure to put on a man. They are doomed from the beginning to not live up to our fairy tale standards.

It is in women's nature to put the man first, or in general, just put others first. IT IS NOT IN A MAN'S NATURE TO DO THAT. Remember that.

A few key points to remember while investing in a serious relationship are as follows:

a) It is imperative that we, as women, retain our own interests. As ridiculous as that sounds, it is crucial to the success of a relationship.

b) Men don't change. The way you meet them is the way they stay.

c) Another biggie—they say things once and they mean it. They don't need to talk about it ten times or affirm their opinion ten times either. We can do that with our friends or anyone else but them.

I have had terrible relationships. Those relationships taught me EVERYTHING I don't want. They helped me to learn about myself—my weaknesses and my strengths. They showed me that for someone to love me, I have to love myself first. I let people treat me like a pile of shit. I am embarrassed that I let people treat me that way. I needed attention and affection so bad that I would suffer through anything to get even a little of it. I figured they were all jerks, so I might as well just date the ones who were jerks from the start. Ridiculous.

Please girls, women of tomorrow, learn from me. Contact me, ask me, or find a friend who can speak the truth to you. Listen to your instincts. If you are questioning someone's actions, then they are probably doing something questionable.

Don't settle until you find someone who makes every day better. Not because he pays the bills or buys you shiny sparkly gifts, but because he is kind and a wonderful companion. Because when he enters a room, you shine. Because his touch gives you tingles.

Always make sure, no matter what, that you can stand on your own two feet. That no matter what happens, you will be okay and are able to be independent. Don't give the reins of your life to anyone else to control—ever.

CHAPTER 2:

TRADITIONAL EDUCATION DOES NOT ALWAYS EQUAL SUCCESS, IT OFTEN EQUALS DEBT.

Let me preface this chapter by saying that I do believe in the value of a quality education and it's ability to get people to the next level in their careers. However, excessive education or unplanned education can be more damaging to a person's financial situation than anything else.

The biggest source of stress and despair for me as a single woman has come from debt. Eighty percent of my debt is directly related to school loans. It has taken me years of running on the hamster wheel of owing more money than I make to face the reality of my situation. I have read books, re-consolidated, researched grants, taken desperate actions and finally one day, it hit me. DON'T SPEND IT IF YOU DON'T HAVE IT.

Do you know what it is like to hate opening the mail? To be so used to overdraft charges that it becomes expected? To get paid and still have a negative checking account? Say hello to my world of my twenties. I repeat that debt and the inability to spend responsibly have been the biggest source of my despair and stress. I spent years blaming others, and the hardest thing to face has been myself and my responsibility. Integrity does not exist unless you can be honest with yourself.

For a long time, I blamed my family. I had no idea how to manage money or what it really took to exist financially in this world. I had never received that education. TRADITIONAL EDUCATION DOES NOT EQUAL SUCCESS.

I spent thousands and thousands of dollars on education and associated costs. Banks and the government just give money away for people to go to school, maybe go to class, possibly graduate, and then land a job that will pay for all the money they borrowed to get through school. Where is the logic in this? It has taken me ten years to figure out that I would have been better off actually learning a SKILL and just working. Why didn't anyone tell me this?

It is embarrassing to admit that there are many basic concepts I do not grasp. I don't understand taxes. I had to learn the hard way about interest rates and credit cards. I don't truly understand how our political system works and am not educated enough about it to even make a good decision when it comes time to vote. I don't understand mortgages or how to buy a home, leaving me to just believe what any realtor or banker tells me. Where were the classes about how to prepare to be an adult? Why did we have to memorize Shakespeare but didn't have classes on how to balance a checkbook or reconcile a bank statement or understand how compound interest can work against you? Really work against you?

Once you are thrown into the workplace, it is too late. I am working sixty hours a week to try and pay back my student loans and associated debt. I don't have time to read books on shit that I should have been taught long ago. What did reading Shakespeare do for me if I can't even make logical investment decisions for my future?

The entire education system should be restructured to teach young adults how to function responsibly in this world. Student loans should not be given out unless an easy to understand (and implement) plan is in place to pay them back.

What would I share with the young women of America?

Well, it seems that the whole country is asking this question.

Choose slowly and wisely. I do believe in continually challenging the learning curve of your mind, which can be done a few hundred dollars at a time. TRY some professions. See if they excite you, if you excel in them, if you like going to work every day. Then continue to invest in the things that will interest you and earn you money. Spending 40,000$ per year for school is just a ridiculous concept and we should NOT be advised to fall into that trap any longer.

Also, it seems that each generation continues to get greedier and greedier. We want things when we are twenty that our parents had to work thirty years to earn. I AM PART OF THAT GENERATION! Now that I am an administrator and am recruiting the youth of America for positions within our company, I see the deterioration of work ethic and the general lack of respect that is rampant in our society today.

Find a great mentor, and then find another. Value the years of experience that those before us have and learn from them.

Take a trip to your bank with someone you trust who has been successful financially. Understand the difference between types of checking, savings, and money markets accounts. Use your ledgers and keep track of what you have and what you spend. As simple as that sounds, most people do not do it!

There are so many resources available to organize your financial profile and to maintain that organization. Keep a daily spending and earning journal. It is very easy to miss the areas where dollar bills just slip out of your hands thanks to debit cards, ATMs, and credit cards.

Again, through a trusted resource, begin to understand investing for the future. Understand that smart decisions NOW will reward you in the future. Understand that paying someone else to invest for you is not always the smartest investment decision. Begin to learn early about real estate, about how to make your money work for you. If I could go back and do one part of my life over, it would have been to follow my own advice here.

I envy those who can comprehend the financial game. I am just beginning to spend wisely now for a well endowed future.

A final note, I do not work anywhere NEAR the field that my degree is in. I borrowed eighty thousand dollars on a six year education that I don't use because I couldn't earn enough in that industry to pay my bills. Hmmmm.

CHAPTER 3:

GET A GOOD
VIBRATOR.

Ah, the vibrator hook and sink 'er line. Oh, what I would do to rewind time and get a REAL sexual education from someone who was honest and straightforward.

Why did they EVER teach us that sex equals love? Why don't they show teenage girls the entire Sex and the City DVD collection in health class?

Hear me, young women of tomorrow, you CAN get STDs and you CAN have unwanted pregnancies and these things WILL affect you for the rest of your lives. I do not intend to make this some shock fest of a book, however, my own experiences have taught me much. I slept with a man who gave me a sexually transmitted disease called moluscum contagiosum. Google that shit. Absolutely horrific. I spent six months visiting the gynecologist having novacaine injected into and around my clitoral area, followed by a scraping of the area. Pause here to imagine that. Pause here to log this into your brain data bank. And check out your man of the month before you jump in the sack.

I had unprotected sex recklessly and spontaneously, and suffered the consequences.

Masturbation is healthy and safe. Understanding your body and researching the best methods for your body are the safest ways to enjoy the wonderfulness of sexual foreplay and intercourse.

What would I share with the young women of America?

Begin at a place like Barnes & Noble, which is where I began my real sexual education. I sat myself in the Sex books aisle and re-visited the section several times. I watched and re-watched and continue to re-watch all of the Sex & the City episodes. That series is my Bible, my truth, and speaks out loud what is like to be a woman in this world of sex with and without love…and how to decipher the difference. I went to a few sex toy parties with some trusted friends and I purchased the Decadent Indulgence 3. I recommend it to all.

I am not opposed to experimenting sexually within relationships. However, I am opposed to trying to fill a void of sadness or loneliness or lack of self worth with sex. Sex with someone who may not care about you and your self worth either. The damage that may ensue is not worth the minutes of pleasure.

There are many types of sexual pleasure in this world and these pleasures can be achieved with and without another person. Save the passion of flesh on flesh for someone who deserves the intimacy of you. The self degradation that occurs due to those who might just toss you aside when they are done, treat you badly in front of others, ignore your phone calls, reject getting to know you and your most wonderful aspects is something not so easily shed from memory.

When you do find love, true love, the wait will have been worth it. Until that time comes, make sure you know that a good vibrator serves the purpose of releasing sexual tension without the baggage of a bad man.

CHAPTER 4:

BELIEVE IN YOURSELF

Believe you can, believe you will, believe in love, believe in yourself, believe in God or some other divine Spirit that will always be there to forgive and to listen and to love unconditionally.

I don't know how to be nice to myself. It has taken me years of being me to recognize when my downward spiral begins and to learn to halt it. I don't know how to say Good Job, Me or Way to Go, Me! I don't know why I never learned to do that. I know how to beat myself up really well though. I know how to tell myself I suck and that I am worse than everyone else. I have always settled for less than I deserve because I never believed I deserved anything. This is the true reason why I am writing this book. I want to let others know who don't believe in themselves, that I believe in them. There is someone out here who accepts you and believes in your dreams. I believe in you.

I have to write down positive things about myself and my life that I read out loud every day. I will read them out loud every day until I believe them and they become real. A wise mentor told me, "The toughest negatives become the most valid positives."

There were many days that the last thought I had before I laid my head down at night was "Please just don't wake me up tomorrow." I lived many years believing that I didn't matter, that if I wasn't here anymore, not one person would be affected. I was twenty seven years old when a complete stranger reached out to me and gave me faith, faith in myself and in other people. The ones who were "supposed" to give me faith, support me, teach me, love me just plain didn't know how to do these things.

What would I share with the young women of America?

So I say to you, young women of the world, if you have moments where you feel completely lost and scared and hopeless—I believe in you. I have had to retrain myself to say nice things to me, to say I CAN do that, I CAN afford that, I AM A SUCCESS, I AM going to be happy and healthy my whole life.

I have compiled my own support group, my own cheering section, my own self help book since high school over the last fifteen years. I refer back to these quotes, pictures, papers, and phrases when I need to remember that I have the power to achieve anything I set my mind to. The following pages are yours. Yours to read in any order you wish and to use or to not use any of the phrases that touch you.

So just do it.

Acknowledge, accept and show compassion and open your heart to others inadequacies. Realize that everyone is doing the best that they can in that moment and judge no one.

Make snow angels or like
my trainer at the gym
says, make sweat angels!

If you can imagine it,
if you can dream it,
you can achieve it!

Remember the great teachers, the ones who really care. Then teach someone something.

Keep things that remind you of why you love someone.

Don't change who you are
for anyone except yourself.

Do unexpected things
for people for no reason
without expecting
anything from them.

Be nice to everyone.

Never give up.

Call your mom and if you
can't call her, write her
a quick note saying hi.

Make the best of what
you have and do not
make yourself miserable
by wishing for what
you have not.

You can never be replaced.

Remember, find a great mentor or two or three.

Play with some kids. And then play with them again. Their innocence and purity can set you free from the weight of your world.

Believe in love.

Believe in Santa Claus—
heck, I still say I would
work for Santa if they
offered me a position in the
North Pole and I would
marry Will Ferrell as Elf.

Take a cheerful view of everything. Never reply in kind to a sharp or angry word, it is the second word that makes the quarrel.

Buy and drink Yogi Tea. It tells you nice things every day you can share with others like "Uplift everybody and uplift yourself."

Help other people,
it will help you.

FINAL WORDS.

FORGIVE AND SAY YOU ARE SORRY.

A friend said to me yesterday, many people forgive but most don't forget. For so many years, I have held on to anger and pain that was over and done the minute it was over. It baffles me that twenty years later, my decisions and reactions can still be affected by incidents from the past. I want to take this time to tell all the people in my life whom I have hurt or let down or was selfish towards that I am sorry. If I gave you my word, and I didn't follow through, I am sorry. My own self pity led me to poor decisions and a lack of integrity. I hope that one day those people come across this book and know that I never meant to hurt them and that I am truly sorry if I did.

CONCLUSION

All I hope to achieve with the words on these pages is that maybe one person who has lost hope will know that there is someone out here who believes in them, who knows they can achieve their dreams, and will listen to them if they need an ear.

In my darkest moments, people reached their hands out to bring me back to the light. I offer you my hand. I believe in you.

www.ingramcontent.com/pod-product-compliance
Lightning Source LLC
Chambersburg PA
CBHW020410290526
45785CB00005B/2494